Vegan Recipes
for Beginners

Prepare tasty plant-based dishes quickly and easily with this wonderful cookbook. Take care of yourself and start eating healthy by eliminating animal-derived foods.

VEGAN LIVING PRESS

Table of Contents

INTRODUCTION

Going vegan is one of the most excellent health benefits for the body, and it is not just the food that you eat but also the active lifestyle. The lifestyle change will encourage you to be more creative in cooking with the vegan diet.

The vegan diet is a plant-based diet that excludes all animal products, including eggs and dairy. This means that followers of the vegan diet only eat vegetables, fruit, grains like rice or quinoa, legumes like beans or lentils, and other plant-based foods such as nuts and seeds. Some forms of the vegan diet also exclude all processed foods, although this is not typical.

The term "vegan" was devised in 1944 by Donald Watson when he co-founded the Vegan Society in England. At first, this meant "non-dairy vegetarian" and later "the doctrine that man should live without exploiting animals.

People who follow a vegan diet are typically motivated by the desire to improve human health and to avoid the cruelty of factory farming. There is also a vital concern for the environment, to reduce pollution and waste, and to be sensitive to animals and the world around us.

Eating vegan has many health benefits - it can reduce the risk of heart disease, certain types of cancer, diabetes, and obesity. It can lower cholesterol levels and blood pressure. For these reasons and more, this diet is being recommended by health professionals worldwide.

Vegan diets contain an adequate amount of protein if enough calories are consumed. It has a wide range of different foods that can provide all the nutrients an average person needs, as long as they avoid vitamin B12 (a nutrient that is produced by bacteria and cannot be synthesized by humans)

In terms of reducing oil, vegan cooking is famous because it requires a lot less oil than traditional recipes. While it may seem impossible to cook without using any oil, many vegan cooks have found ways to make the most from a minimal amount of oil.

Veganism is on the rapid rise, and for a good reason! These beautiful cookbooks offer not only an alternative to meat, chicken, and fish but also a delicious one. They are perfect for adding more plant-based foods to their diet or are vegan already. You'll find mouthwatering recipes from breakfast through dessert that make these cookbooks a must-have for any foodie.

BREAKFAST

WALNUT CRUNCH BANANA BREAD

Preparation Time: 5 minutes

Cooking Time: 1 hr. 30 min

Servings: 1 loaf

INGREDIENTS

- ✓ 4 ripe bananas
- ✓ ½ teaspoon baking soda
- ✓ 1½ cups whole-wheat flour
- ✓ 1 tablespoon apple cider vinegar
- ✓ 1 teaspoon vanilla extract
- ✓ ¼ cup maple syrup
- ✓ ½ teaspoon ground cinnamon
- ✓ ¼ cup walnut pieces (optional)

PREPARATION

1. Preheat the oven to 350°F.
2. In an enormous container, use a fork to mash the bananas until they reach a puréed consistency. Add and stir the maple syrup, apple cider vinegar, and vanilla.

3. Stir in the flour, cinnamon, and baking soda. Fold in the walnut pieces (if using).
4. Carefully pour the batter into a loaf pan, filling it three-quarters full. Bake until you can stick a knife into the middle and it comes out clean or for 1 hour.
5. Pull out of the oven and give it time to cool for a minimum of 30 minutes before serving.

NUTRITION

Calories: 178; Total fat: 1g; Carbohydrates: 40g; Fiber: 5g; Protein: 4g

SAVORY PANCAKES

Preparation Time: 10 minutes

Cooking time: 15minutes

Servings: 4

INGREDIENTS

- ✓ 1 cup whole-wheat flour
- ✓ 1 teaspoon garlic salt
- ✓ 2 cups tightly packed greens (arugula, spinach, or baby kale work great)
- ✓ 1/2 teaspoon baking soda
- ✓ 1/2 cup finely chopped mushrooms
- ✓ 1 cup lightly pressed, crumbled soft or firm tofu
- ✓ 1/2 cup unsweetened plant-based milk
- ✓ 1/4 teaspoon salt
- ✓ 1/4 cup lemon juice
- ✓ 2 tablespoons extra-virgin olive oil
- ✓ 1/2 cup finely chopped onion
- ✓ 1 teaspoon onion powder

PREPARATION

1. Attach the flour, garlic salt, onion powder, baking soda, and salt. Mix well. In a blender, combine the tofu, plant-based milk, lemon juice, and olive oil. Purée at high speed for 30 seconds.

2. Transfer into a container of dry ingredients and whisk until combined well. Fold in the mushrooms, onion, and greens.

NUTRITION

Calories: 132; Fat: 10g; Protein: 12g; Carbohydrates: 44g; Fiber: 9g; Sugar: 1g; Sodium: 254mg

TOFU-SPINACH SCRAMBLE

Preparation Time: 15 minutes

Cooking time: 20minutes

Servings: 5

INGREDIENTS

- ✓ 1 small yellow onion, diced
- ✓ 3 teaspoons minced garlic (about 3 cloves)
- ✓ 3 large celery stalks, chopped
- ✓ 2 large carrots, peeled (optional) and chopped
- ✓ 1 (14-ounce) package water-packed extra-firm tofu
- ✓ 1 teaspoon chili powder
- ✓ 5 cups loosely packed spinach
- ✓ 1/2 teaspoon ground turmeric
- ✓ 1/2 teaspoon salt (optional)
- ✓ 1/4 teaspoon freshly ground black pepper
- ✓ 1/2 teaspoon ground cumin
- ✓ 1 teaspoon extra-virgin olive oil or 1/4 cup vegetable broth

PREPARATION

1. Drain the tofu by placing it, wrapped in a paper towel, on a plate in the sink. Place a cutting board over the tofu, then set a heavy pot, can, or cookbook on the cutting board. Remove after 10 minutes. (Alternatively, use a tofu press.)

2. In a medium bowl, crumble the tofu with your hands or a potato masher.

3. Heat the olive oil. Add the onion, garlic, celery, carrots, and sauté for 5 minutes until the onion is softened.

4. Add the crumbled tofu, chili powder, cumin, turmeric, salt (if using), and pepper, and continue cooking for 7 to 8 more minutes, frequently stirring, until the tofu begins to brown.

5. Add the spinach and mix well. Cover and reduce the heat to medium. Steam the spinach for 3 minutes.

6. Divide equally among 5 single-serving containers. Let cool before sealing the lids.

NUTRITION

Calories: 122; Protein: 14g; Carbohydrates: 54g; Fat: 15g; Fiber: 8g; Sugar: 1g

SMOOTHIE BREAKFAST BOWL

Preparation Time: 10 minutes

Cooking time: 20minutes

Servings: 4

INGREDIENTS

- ✓ 4 peeled bananas
- ✓ 4 cups plant-based milk
- ✓ 1 cup dragon fruit or fruit of choice
- ✓ 2 cups fresh berries
- ✓ 1/2 cup slivered almonds
- ✓ 1 cup Baked Granola

PREPARATION

1. Open 4 quart-size, freezer-safe bags, and layer in the following order: 1 banana (halved or sliced) and 1/4 cup dragon fruit.

2. Into 4 small jelly jars, layer in the following order: 1/4 cup granola, 1/2 cup berries, and 2 tablespoons slivered almonds.

3. To serve, take a frozen bag of bananas and dragon fruit and transfer it to a blender. Add 1 cup of plant-based milk, and blend until smooth. Pour into a container. Add the contents of 1 jar of granola, berries, and almonds over the smoothie's top and serve with a spoon.

NUTRITION

Calories: 109; Fat: 12g; Protein: 24g; Carbohydrates: 24g; Fiber: 8g; Sugar: 5g; Sodium: 366mg

QUINOA BREAKFAST PORRIDGE

Preparation Time: 10 minutes

Cooking time: 5 minutes

Servings: 3

INGREDIENTS

- ✓ 1 cup dry quinoa
- ✓ 1 tablespoon ground flax meal
- ✓ 1/2 tsp. vanilla
- ✓ 1/2 tsp. cinnamon
- ✓ 1 tbsp. agave or maple syrup
- ✓ 2 cups almond milk

PREPARATION

1. Combine quinoa, almond milk, sugar, vanilla, and cinnamon in a bit of pot.
2. Heat to the point of boiling and lessen to a stew.
3. Allow the quinoa to cook until most of the fluid is retained and quinoa is fleecy (15-20 minutes).
4. Blend in the flax meal. Blend in any extra toppers or include INS, and enjoy.

NUTRITION

Calories: 122; Fat: 12g; Protein: 12g; Fiber: 9g; Sugar: 5g; Sodium: 154mg Carbohydrates: 34g

BARLEY BREAKFAST BOWL

Preparation Time: 5 minutes

Cooking time: 15minutes

Servings: 4

INGREDIENTS

- ✓ 1.1/2 cups pearl barley
- ✓ 3 cups sweetened vanilla plant-based milk
- ✓ 1.1/2 cups dried cranberries
- ✓ Large pinch of salt
- ✓ 2 tablespoons slivered almonds (optional)
- ✓ 3.3/4 cups water

PREPARATION

1. Put the barley, water, and salt. Bring to a boil.
2. Divide the barley into 6 jars or single-serving storage containers. I attached the 1/4 cup of dried cranberries to each. Pour 1/2 cup of plant-based milk into each.
3. Attached the 1 teaspoon of slivered almonds (if using) to each. Close the jars tightly with lids.

NUTRITION

Calories: 109; Fat: 15g; Fiber: 8g; Sugar: 1g; Sodium: 466mg; Carbohydrates: 32g; Protein: 24g;

PUMPKIN STEEL-CUT OATS

Preparation Time: 15 minutes

Cooking time: 25 minutes

Servings: 4

INGREDIENTS

- ✓ 3 cups water
- ✓ 2 tablespoons maple syrup
- ✓ 1/4 cup pumpkin seeds (pipits)
- ✓ 1 cup steel-cut oats
- ✓ 1/2 cup canned pumpkin purée
- ✓ Pinch salt

PREPARATION

1. Whip and reduce the heat to low. Simmer until the oats are soft, 20 to 30 minutes, continuing to stir occasionally.
2. Stir in the pumpkin purée and continue cooking on low for 3 to 5 minutes longer. Add and Stir in the pumpkin seeds and maple syrup, and season with the salt to taste.
3. Divide the oatmeal into 4 single-serving containers. Let cool before sealing the lids.

NUTRITION

Calories: 132; Fat: 19; Protein: 4535g; Sugar: 15 g; Carbohydrates: 75g; Fiber: 73 g; Sodium: 345mg

CINNAMON AND SPICE OVERNIGHT OATS

Preparation Time: 15 minutes

Cooking time: 20 minutes

Servings: 3

INGREDIENTS

- ✓ 5 tablespoons pumpkin seeds (pipits)
- ✓ 5 tablespoons chopped pecans
- ✓ 1/2 to 1 teaspoon ground ginger
- ✓ 2 1/2 cups old-fashioned rolled oats
- ✓ 2 1/2 teaspoons maple syrup or agave syrup
- ✓ 1/2 to 1 teaspoon ground cinnamon
- ✓ 5 cups unsweetened plant-based milk
- ✓ 1/2 to 1 teaspoon salt

PREPARATION

1. Line up 5 wide-mouth pint jars. In each pot, combine 1/2 cup of oats, 1 tablespoon of pumpkin seeds, 1 tablespoon of pecans, 1 cup of plant-based milk, 1/2 teaspoon of maple syrup, 1 pinch of salt, 1 pinch of cinnamon, and 1 pinch of ginger.

2. Stir the ingredients in each jar. Close the jars tightly with lids.

3.   To serve, top with fresh fruit (if using).

NUTRITION

Calories: 124; Protein: 35g; Fiber: 65 g; Carbohydrates: 80; Sugar: 18 g Sodium: 276

LUNCH

ROASTED VEGGIES IN LEMON SAUCE

Preparation Time: 15 minutes

Cooking Time: 20 minutes

Servings: 5

INGREDIENTS

- ✓ 2 cloves garlic, sliced
- ✓ 2 teaspoons lemon zest
- ✓ 1 .1/2 cups cauliflower florets
- ✓ 1 tablespoon olive oil
- ✓ 3/4 cup zucchini, diced
- ✓ 1 .1/2 cups broccoli florets
- ✓ 1 teaspoon dried oregano, crushed
- ✓ 3/4 cup red bell pepper, diced
- ✓ Salt to taste

PREPARATION

1. Readily heat your oven to 425 degrees F.

2. Merge the garlic, broccoli, and cauliflower.

3. Put in the oil and season with salt and oregano.

4. Roast in the oven for 10 minutes.

5. Attach the zucchini and bell pepper to the pan.

6. Stir well.

7. Roast for another 10 minutes.

8. Sprinkle lemon zest on top before serving.

9. Fill into a food container and reheat before serving.

<u>NUTRITION</u>

Calories 52; Sodium 134 mg; Fat 3 g; Carbohydrate 5 g; Fiber 2 g; Protein 2 g; Sugars 2 g

VEGAN TACOS

Preparation Time: 20 minutes

Cooking Time: 10 minutes

Servings: 4

INGREDIENTS

- ✓ 16 oz. tofu drained and crumbled
- ✓ 1 teaspoon chili powder
- ✓ 1/2 teaspoon garlic powder
- ✓ 2 tablespoons tamari
- ✓ 1/2 teaspoon onion powder
- ✓ 1 tablespoon olive oil
- ✓ 1 ripe avocado
- ✓ 2 cups iceberg lettuce, shredded
- ✓ Salt to taste
- ✓ Pickled radishes
- ✓ 8 corn tortillas, warmed
- ✓ 1/2 cup fresh salsa
- ✓ 1 tablespoon vegan mayonnaise
- ✓ 1 teaspoon lime juice

PREPARATION

1. Merge all the ingredients in a bowl.

2. Soak the tofu in the mixture for 10 minutes.

3. Pour the oil into a pan over medium heat.

4. Cook the tofu mixture for 10 minutes.

5. In another bowl, mash the avocado and mix with mayo, lime juice, and salt.

6. Stuff each corn tortilla with tofu mixture, mashed avocado, salsa, and lettuce.

7. Serve with pickled radishes.

NUTRITION

Calories 360; Sodium 610 mg; Fat 21 g; Fiber 8 g; Sugars 4 g; Protein 17 g; Carbohydrate 33 g

TOFU SHARMA RICE

Preparation Time: 15 minutes

Cooking Time: 15 minutes

Servings: 4

INGREDIENTS

- ✓ 4 cups cooked tofu, sliced into small cubes
- ✓ 4 cups cooked brown rice
- ✓ Hot sauce
- ✓ 4 cups cucumber, cubed
- ✓ 4 cups tomatoes, cubed
- ✓ 2 cups cabbage, shredded
- ✓ 1/8 cup garlic, minced
- ✓ Garlic salt to taste
- ✓ 1/2 cup vegan mayo
- ✓ 4 cups white onion, cubed

PREPARATION

1. Add brown rice into 4 food containers.
2. Arrange tofu, cucumber, tomatoes, white onion, and cabbage on top.

3. In a bowl, mix the mayo, garlic, and garlic salt.

4. Drizzle on top with garlic sauce and hot sauce before serving.

NUTRITION

Calories 667; Fat 12.6g; Sodium 95mg; Carb 116.5g; Fiber 9.9g; Sugars 9.4g; Protein 26.1g

GRILLED SUMMER VEGGIES

Preparation Time: 15 minutes

Cooking Time: 6 minutes

Servings: 6

INGREDIENTS

- ✓ 2 teaspoons cider vinegar
- ✓ 1 tablespoon olive oil
- ✓ 1 eggplant, sliced crosswise
- ✓ 1 teaspoon fresh parsley, chopped
- ✓ 1 tablespoon cider vinegar
- ✓ 1 onion, sliced into wedges
- ✓ 2 red bell peppers, sliced
- ✓ 3 tablespoons olive oil
- ✓ 3 tomatoes, sliced in half
- ✓ 6 large mushrooms, stems removed
- ✓ 1/4 teaspoon fresh rosemary, chopped
- ✓ 1/4 teaspoon fresh thyme, chopped
- ✓ Salt and pepper to taste

PREPARATION

1. Merge the vinegar, oil, thyme, parsley, rosemary, salt, and pepper to make the dressing.
2. In a container, mix the onion, red bell pepper, tomatoes, mushrooms, and eggplant.
3. Toss in remaining olive oil and cider vinegar.
4. Grill over medium heat for 3 minutes.
5. Turn the vegetables and grill for another 3 minutes.
6. Arrange grilled vegetables in a food container.
7. Drizzle with the herbed mixture when ready to serve.

NUTRITION

Calories 127; Sodium 55 mg; Carbohydrate 11 g; Fiber 5 g; Sugars 5 g; Protein 3 g; Fat 9 g

BURRITO & CAULIFLOWER RICE BOWL

Preparation Time: 15 minutes

Cooking Time: 10 minutes

Servings: 4

INGREDIENTS

- ✓ 1 cup avocado, diced
- ✓ 12 oz. frozen cauliflower rice
- ✓ 1 cup cooked tofu cubes
- ✓ 1/4 cup fresh cilantro, chopped
- ✓ 1 teaspoon unsalted taco seasoning
- ✓ 1/2 cup salsa
- ✓ 1 cup red cabbage, sliced thinly
- ✓ 4 teaspoons olive oil

PREPARATION

1. Prepare cauliflower rice according to directions in the package.
2. Toss cauliflower rice in olive oil and taco seasoning.
3. Divide among 4 food containers with lid.
4. Top with tofu, cabbage, salsa, and cilantro.

5. Cover the container and cool in the refrigerator until ready to serve.

6. Before serving, add avocado slices.

NUTRITION

Calories 298; Fat 20 g; Protein 15 g; Sodium 680 mg; Carbohydrate 15 g; Fiber 6 g; Sugars 5 g

SUPERFOOD BUDDHA BOWL

Preparation Time: 10 minutes

Cooking Time: 10 minutes

Servings: 4

INGREDIENTS

- ✓ 2 tablespoons lemon juice
- ✓ 1 cup frozen shelled edam me (thawed)
- ✓ 1/2 cup hummus
- ✓ 5 oz. baby kale
- ✓ 8 oz. cooked baby beets, sliced
- ✓ 8 oz. microwavable quinoa
- ✓ 1/4 cup sunflower seeds, toasted
- ✓ 1 cup pecans
- ✓ 2 tablespoons flaxseeds
- ✓ 1 avocado, sliced
- ✓ Water

PREPARATION

1. Cook quinoa according to directions in the packaging.
2. Set aside and let cool.

3.   In a bowl, mix the lemon juice and hummus.

4.   Add water to achieve desired consistency.

5.   Divide mixture into 4 condiment containers.

6.   Cover containers with lids and put them in the refrigerator.

7.   Divide the baby kale into 4 food containers with lids.

8.   Top with quinoa, beets, Edam me, and sunflower seeds.

9.   Place in the refrigerator until it's ready.

NUTRITION

Calories 381; Fat 19 g; Sodium 188 mg; Carbohydrate 43 g; Fiber 13 g; Protein 16 g; Sugars 8 g

RISOTTO WITH TOMATO & HERBS

Preparation Time: 10 minutes

Cooking Time: 20 minutes

Servings: 32

INGREDIENTS

- ✓ 2 oz. Arborio rice
- ✓ 1 teaspoon dried garlic, minced
- ✓ 3 tablespoons dried onion, minced
- ✓ 1 tablespoon dried Italian seasoning, crushed
- ✓ 3/4 cup snipped dried tomatoes

PREPARATION

1. Make the dry risotto mix by combining all the ingredients except broth in a large bowl.
2. Divide the mixture into eight resealable plastic bags. Seal the bag.
3. Store at room temperature for up to 3 months.
4. Serve by pouring the broth into a pot.
5. Add the contents of 1 plastic bag of dry risotto mix.
6. Then boil and reduce the heat.

7.   Bring with vegetables.

NUTRITION

Calories 80 Protein 3 g Sodium 276 mg Carbohydrate 17 g Fiber 2 g

SPINACH WITH WALNUTS & AVOCADO

Preparation Time: 5 minutes

Cooking Time: 0 minute

Servings: 1

INGREDIENTS

- ✓ 3 cups baby spinach
- ✓ 1/2 cup strawberries, sliced
- ✓ 1 tablespoon white onion, chopped
- ✓ 2 tablespoons vinaigrette
- ✓ 1/4 medium avocado, diced
- ✓ 2 tablespoons walnut, toasted

PREPARATION

1. Put the spinach, strawberries, and onion in a glass jar with a lid.
2. Drizzle dressing on top.
3. Top with avocado and walnuts.
4. Shut down the lid and refrigerate until ready to serve.

NUTRITION

Calories 296 Protein 8 g; Carb 27 g; Sodium 195 mg; Fat 18 g;
Fiber 10 g; Sugars 11 g

DINNER

BAKED BRUSSELS SPROUTS

Preparation Time: 10minutes

Cooking time: 40minutes

Servings: 4

INGREDIENTS

- ✓ 1 pound Brussels sprouts
- ✓ 1 tablespoon balsamic vinegar
- ✓ 2 teaspoons extra-virgin olive or canola oil
- ✓ 4 teaspoons minced garlic (about 4 cloves)
- ✓ 1/2 teaspoon salt
- ✓ 1/4 teaspoon freshly ground black pepper
- ✓ 1 teaspoon dried oregano
- ✓ 1/2 teaspoon dried rosemary

PREPARATION

1. Preheat the oven to 400ºF.
2. Trim and halve the Brussels sprouts. Transfer to a large bowl. Toss with olive oil, garlic, oregano, rosemary, salt, and pepper to coat well.

3. Transfer to the prepared baking sheet. Bake for 35 to 40 minutes, shake the pan occasionally to help, until crisp on the outside and tender on the inside.

4. Pull from the oven and place in a large container. Stir in the balsamic vinegar, coating well.

5. Divide the Brussels sprouts evenly among 4 single-serving containers. Let cool before sealing the lids.

NUTRITION

Calories: 128 Protein 18g   Protein: 10g Fat: 50g Carbs: 23g Fibers: 5g

MISO SPAGHETTI SQUASH

Preparation Time: 5minutes

Cooking time: 50minutes

Servings: 4

INGREDIENTS

- ✓ 1 (3-pound) spaghetti squash
- ✓ 1 tablespoon white miso
- ✓ 1 tablespoon unseasoned rice vinegar
- ✓ 1 tablespoon hot water

PREPARATION

1. Preheat the oven.
2. Peel the squash, cut-side down, on the prepared baking sheet. Bake until tender for 35 to 40 minutes,
3. Cool the squash until it is easy to handle. With a fork, scrape out the flesh, which will be stringy, like spaghetti. Transfer to a large bowl.
4. In a small container, combine the hot water, vinegar, and miso with a whisk or fork. Pour over the squash. Gently toss with tongs to coat the squash.

5. Divide the squash evenly among 4 single-serving containers. Let cool before sealing the lids.

6. Storage: Place in the refrigerator for up to 1 week or freeze for up to 4 months. To thaw, refrigerate overnight. Preheat in a microwave for 2 to 3 minutes.

NUTRITION

Calories: 120 Protein: 10g Fat: 16g Carbs: 79g Fibers: 5g

LASAGNA SOUP

Preparation time: 5 minutes

Cooking time: 30 minutes

SERVINGS: 5

INGREDIENTS

- ✓ 2 cups Vegetable broth
- ✓ 8 ounces Portobello mushrooms, gills removed and finely diced
- ✓ 1 teaspoon Onion powder
- ✓ 28 ounces Crushed tomatoes
- ✓ 28 ounces Diced tomatoes
- ✓ 2 tablespoons Olive oil
- ✓ 4 cloves Garlic, minced
- ✓ 33 cups Basil, fresh, chopped
- ✓ 2 tablespoons Nutritional yeast –
- ✓ 1 teaspoon Sea salt
- ✓ 8 ounces Lentil Lasagna noodles (Explore Cuisine)
- ✓ .66 cup Vegan mozzarella shreds -
- ✓ 1 teaspoon Thyme, dried

PREPARATION

1. Pour the olive oil and allow it to heat over medium-high. Add in the diced mushrooms and cook while stirring regularly for eight minutes.

2. Pour the diced tomatoes, garlic, and basil into the pot and continue to cook for four minutes.

3. Into the soup pot, add the crushed tomatoes, onion powder, thyme, nutritional yeast, and vegetable broth. Bring this mixture to a boil.

4. Crack the lasagna noodles into small pieces and add them to the pot. Reduce the heat, fit on a lid, and allow the soup to simmer on low for twenty minutes.

5. Serve the soup topped with vegan mozzarella shreds.

NUTRITION

Calories: 134 Fiber: 9g Sodium: 118mg fat: 9g Carbs: 19g Protein: 6g

ROASTED MEXICAN-SPICED CAULIFLOWER

Preparation Time: 10minutes

Cooking time: 25minutes

Servings: 5

INGREDIENTS

1 head cauliflower, cut into bite-size florets

2 tablespoons olive oil

4 garlic cloves, sliced

2 scallions, thinly sliced, for garnish

1 tablespoon Taco Seasoning or store-bought taco seasoning

1/2 cup fresh corn kernels

PREPARATION

1.   Preheat the oven to 425°F. Line a baking sheet with parchment paper.

2.   Merge the cauliflower, corn, garlic, oil, and taco seasoning. Spread the cauliflower mixture evenly on the prepared baking sheet.

3.   Bake for 15 minutes, toss with a spatula, and bake for an additional 10 minutes, or until the cauliflower has gotten

darker and browned slightly on the edges. Serve garnished with scallions.

NUTRITION

Calories: 134; Fat: 9g; Protein: 121g; Total carbs: 10g; Net carbs: 232g; Fiber: 7g; Sodium: 434mg Sugar: 14

VEGGIE SOUP (INSTANT POT)

Preparation time: 5 minutes

Cooking time: 10 minutes

Servings: 4

INGREDIENTS

- ✓ 2 tbsp. olive oil
- ✓ 1 onion (medium, chopped)
- ✓ 3 tbsp. parsley (fresh, minced)
- ✓ 1 clove of garlic (minced)
- ✓ 3 (14.5 oz.) cans vegetable broth
- ✓ 4 cups tomatoes (chopped)
- ✓ 1 cup celery (chopped)
- ✓ 1 cup carrots (sliced)
- ✓ 1 zucchini (halved and sliced)
- ✓ 2 tsp. basil (dried, crushed)
- ✓ 1/2 tsp. salt
- ✓ 1/2 tsp. Italian seasoning
- ✓ 1 tsp. red pepper flakes (crushed)
- ✓ 5 cups kale leaves (chopped)

PREPARATION

1. Heat the pot on "sauté" mode until it says "hot"; then adds the oil.

2. Attach the onion, and cook until it is tender. Add the parsley and garlic, constantly stirring for 30 seconds; then add the vegetable broth.

3. Stir in the celery, tomato, zucchini, carrots, Italian seasoning, and red pepper to the pot and turn off the heat. Close the lid.

4. Turn the steam option to "sealing," selecting high pressure for 6 minutes. When done, turn the cooker off again, choosing the quick pressure release option; then select "sauté."

5. Add kale, stirring for 3 minutes or so until the soup comes to a boil. Turn the cooker off and serve.

NUTRITION

Calories: 134 Carbs: 26g Protein: 6g Fiber: 8g Sodium: 138mg fat: 9g

THE ATHENA PIZZA

Preparation time: 10minutes

Cooking time: 15minutes

Servings: 3

INGREDIENTS:

- ✓ 4 Pita Bread rounds or store-bought pita bread
- ✓ 6 cups lightly packed stemmed and thinly sliced kale
- ✓ 1 tablespoon extra-virgin olive oil
- ✓ 1 recipe Macadamia-Rosemary Cheese
- ✓ 2 tablespoons freshly squeezed lemon juice
- ✓ 1/4 teaspoon sea salt
- ✓ 1 cup halved grape or cherry tomatoes
- ✓ 4 garlic cloves, finely minced or pressed
- ✓ 1/2 cup pitted, chopped Klamath olives

PREPARATION

1. Preheat the oven to 400°F.
2. Arrange the pita bread rounds in a single layer on two large rimmed baking sheets. Bake for 5 to 10 minutes until golden brown and crisp. Remove and set aside.

3. In a large bowl, mix the kale, lemon juice, and olive oil. Using your hands, work the lemon and oil into the kale, squeezing firmly so that the kale becomes soft and tenderized, as well as a darker shade of green. Stir in the garlic and salt.

4. .Assemble the pizzas by spreading each pita with a generous coating of macadamia cheese and topping evenly with the kale salad, tomatoes, and olives.

NUTRITION

Calories: 537; Protein: 82g; Sodium: 446; Fat: 19g; fat: 7g

GREEK FLATBREADS

Preparation time: 15minutes

Cooking time: 10minutes

Servings: 4

INGREDIENTS

- ✓ 4 Pita Bread rounds or store-bought pita rounds
- ✓ 1/2 cup pitted, halved Klamath olives
- ✓ 2 cups baby spinach leaves
- ✓ 1/2 cup thinly sliced red onion
- ✓ 1 cup sliced grape tomatoes
- ✓ 1/3 cup thinly sliced fresh basil
- ✓ 1/4 cup sliced Greek pepperoncini (optional)
- ✓ 3 tablespoons extra-virgin olive oil (optional)

PREPARATION

1. Preheat the oven to 350°F.

2. Set the pita rounds on the oven rack and bake for 5 to 10 minutes until lightly browned and crisp.

3. Place a pita on each plate. Spread the hummus evenly over each. Evenly distribute the spinach, tomatoes, olives, onion, basil, and pepperoncini (if using) on top.
4. Drizzle with olive oil (if using), then cut into quarters and serve immediately.

NUTRITION

Calories: 437; Sodium: 346; Protein: 82g; fat: 7g

MEDITERRANEAN MACRO PLATE

Preparation time: 10minutes

Cooking time: 10minutes

Servings: 4

INGREDIENTS

- ✓ 6 cups cauliflower florets
- ✓ 8 ounces firm or extra-firm tofu
- ✓ Olive oil cooking spray
- ✓ 1 tablespoon herbs de Provence
- ✓ Sea salt
- ✓ 1 recipe Full Madams
- ✓ 1 recipe Happy Hummus
- ✓ 6 cups sliced cucumber

PREPARATION

1. Spout an inch of water into a large pot and insert a steamer rack. Boil the water, add the cauliflower, cover, and cook over medium heat until tender, about 10 minutes.

2.   While the cauliflower is cooking, cut the tofu into 1-inch cubes. Heat a large skillet over medium-high heat.

3.   Spray with cooking spray and lay the tofu in a single layer in the skillet. Sprinkle evenly with the herbs de Provence and salt.

4.   Cook until the undersides are golden brown or for 4 minutes. Spray with cooking spray, flip, and cook for an additional 3 to 4 minutes until golden brown on the other side. Remove from the heat.

5.   Divide the full me dames and hummus among 6 plates. Add a scoop of tofu and cauliflower to each dish and divide the cucumber for dipping into the hummus.

6.   Serve immediately.

NUTRITION

Calories: 537, Protein: 82g, fat: 7g Sodium: 446, Fat: 19g

SNACKS

TORTILLA CHIPS

Preparation Time: 10 minutes

Cooking time: 4 minutes

Servings: 4

INGREDIENTS

- ✓ Eight corn tortillas, each cut into triangles
- ✓ Salt and black pepper to the taste
- ✓ 1 tbsp. olive oil

PREPARATION

1. Brush tortilla chips with the oil, place them in your air fryer's basket and cook for 4 minutes at 400 degrees F
2. Serve them with salt and pepper sprinkled all over.
3. Enjoy!

NUTRITION

Calories 53g, Carbs 10g, Protein 2 g, Fat 1g, Fiber 1.5g

BEETS CHIPS

Preparation Time: 10 minutes

Cooking time: 20 minutes

Servings: 4

INGREDIENTS

- ✓ Four medium beets, peeled and cut into skinny slices
- ✓ 1 tbsp. chives, chopped
- ✓ Salt and black pepper to the taste
- ✓ Cooking spray

PREPARATION

1. Arrange beets chips in your air fryer's basket, grease with cooking spray, season with salt and black pepper, cook them at 350 degrees F for 20 minutes, flipping them halfway, transfer to bowls and serve with chives sprinkled on top as a snack
2. Enjoy!

NUTRITION

Calories 80, Carbs 6g, Protein 1g, Fat 1g, Fiber 2g

RICE BALLS

Preparation Time: 10 minutes

Cooking time: 35 minutes

Servings: 6

INGREDIENTS

- ✓ 1 cup Arborio rice
- ✓ 1 cup veggie stock
- ✓ 1 tbsp. olive oil
- ✓ Marinara sauce for serving
- ✓ One small yellow onion, chopped
- ✓ 2 ounces tofu, cubed
- ✓ ¼ cup sun-dried tomatoes, chopped
- ✓ One and ½ cups vegan breadcrumbs
- ✓ A drizzle of olive oil
- ✓ Salt and black pepper to the taste

PREPARATION

1. Heat a pan with 1 tbsp. oil over moderate heat, add onion, stir and cook for 5 minutes.

2. Add rice, stock, salt, and pepper, stir, cook on low heat for 20 minutes, spread on a baking sheet, and leave aside to cool down.

3. Transfer rice to a bowl, add tomatoes and half of the breadcrumbs and stir well.

4. Shape 12 balls, press a hole in each ball, stuff with tofu cubes, and mold them again.

5. Coat them in the remaining breadcrumbs, arrange all balls in your air fryer, drizzle the oil over them and cook at 380 degrees F for 10 minutes.

6. Flip them and cook for 5 minutes more.

7. Arrange them on a plate and then serve them as a snack.

NUTRITION

Calories 137, Fat 12g, Fiber 1g, Carbs 7g, Protein 5g

BANANA CHIPS

Preparation time: 10 minutes

Cooking time: 10 minutes

Servings: 4

INGREDIENTS

- ✓ A drizzle of olive oil
- ✓ A pinch of black pepper

PREPARATION

1. Four bananas, peeled and sliced into thin pieces
2. Put banana slices in the air fryer, drizzle the oil, season with pepper, toss to coat gently, and air fry at 360 degrees for 10 minutes.
3. Serve as a snack.
4. Enjoy!

NUTRITION

Calories 100, Carbs 20g, Protein 1 g, Fat 7g, Fiber 1g

CABBAGE ROLLS

Preparation Time: 10 minutes

Cooking time: 25 minutes

Servings: 8

INGREDIENTS

- ✓ Two yellow onions, chopped
- ✓ 1 tsp. coconut aminos
- ✓ ½ red bell pepper, chopped
- ✓ 2 tbsp. Corn flour mixed with 1 tbsp. water
- ✓ One carrot, chopped
- ✓ 2 cups cabbage, chopped
- ✓ 1-inch piece ginger, grated
- ✓ Eight garlic cloves, minced
- ✓ Salt and black pepper to the taste
- ✓ 2 tbsp. olive oil
- ✓ Ten vegan spring roll sheets
- ✓ Cooking spray

PREPARATION

1. Add and heat the oil in a pan over medium-high heat, add cabbage, onions, carrots, bell pepper, ginger, garlic, salt, pepper, and amino, stir, cook for 4 minutes. Take off the heat.
2. Cut each spring roll sheet and cut it into four pieces.
3. Place 1 tbsp. Veggie mix in one corner, roll, and fold edges.
4. Repeat this with the remaining rolls, place them in the air fryer's basket, grease them with cooking oil and cook at 360 degrees F for 10 minutes on each side.
5. Arrange on a plate and then serve as an appetizer.
6. Enjoy!

NUTRITION

Calories 150, Fat 3g, Fiber 4g, Carbs 7g, Protein 2g

POTATO CHIPS

Preparation Time: 30 minutes

Cooking time: 30 minutes

Servings: 4

INGREDIENTS

- ✓ 2 tsp. rosemary, chopped
- ✓ 1 tbsp. olive oil
- ✓ A pinch of sea salt
- ✓ Four potatoes, scrubbed, peeled, and cut into thin strips

PREPARATION

1.   In a container, mix potato chips with salt and oil, toss to coat, place them in your air fryer's basket and cook at 330 degrees F for 30 minutes.

2.   Divide them into bowls, sprinkle rosemary all over, and serve as a snack.

3.   Enjoy!

NUTRITION

Calories 200, Fat 4g, Fiber 4g, Carbs 14g, Protein 5g

CHICKPEAS SNACK

Preparation Time: 10 minutes

Cooking time: 20 minutes

Servings: 4

INGREDIENTS

- ✓ 15 ounces canned chickpeas, drained
- ✓ ½ tsp. cumin, ground
- ✓ 1 tbsp. olive oil
- ✓ 1 tsp. smoked paprika
- ✓ Salt and black pepper to the taste

PREPARATION

1. In a container, mix chickpeas with oil, cumin, paprika, salt, and pepper, toss to coat, place them in the fryer's basket, cook at 390 degrees F for 10 minutes, and transfer a bowl.
2. Serve as a snack
3. Enjoy!

NUTRITION

Calories 140, Fat 1g, Fiber 6g, Carbs 20g, Protein 6g

APPLE CHIPS

Preparation Time: 10 minutes

Cooking time: 15 minutes

Servings: 2

INGREDIENTS

- ✓ 1 tbsp. stevia
- ✓ ½ tsp. cinnamon powder
- ✓ One apple, cored and thinly sliced

PREPARATION

1. Arrange apple slices in your air fryer's basket, add stevia and cinnamon, toss and cook at 390 degrees F for 10 minutes, turning them halfway.
2. Transfer to the container and serve as a snack.
3. Enjoy!

NUTRITION

Calories 90, Fiber 4g, Carbs 12g, Protein 4 g

DESSERTS

VANILLA MUG CAKE

Preparation Time: 1 Minute

Cooking Time: 4 minutes

Servings: 1

INGREDIENTS

- ✓ ¼ cup Cashew Milk
- ✓ ¼ tsp. Vanilla Extract
- ✓ 1 scoop Vanilla Protein Powder
- ✓ 1 tbsp. Granulated Sweetener of your choice
- ✓ 1 tbsp. Coconut Flour
- ✓ ½ tsp. Baking Powder
- ✓ 1 tsp. Chocolate Chips

PREPARATION

1. Start by applying baking spray all over a microwave-safe mug.

2. To this, stir in the protein powder, coconut flour, baking powder, and granulated sweetener. Mix well.

3. Now, pour the cashew milk into the flour mixture along with vanilla extract. Tip: At this point, if the combination

seems crumbly, add more milk to it until you get a thick batter.

4. Next, cook in the microwave for 1 minute or until the center is set and cooked.

5. Serve and enjoy.

NUTRITION

Calories: 170cal Proteins: 29g Carbohydrates: 7g Fat: 6g

FRUITS AND BERRIES IN ORANGE JUICE SALAD

Preparation Time: 10 minutes

Cooking Time: 0 minute

Servings: 2

INGREDIENTS

- ✓ 1 cup strawberries
- ✓ 1 cup of orange juice
- ✓ 1 cup sweet cherries
- ✓ 1/2 cup of blueberries
- ✓ 1 kiwi
- ✓ 1 peach
- ✓ 1 red apple
- ✓ 2 tablespoons lemon juice

PREPARATION

1. Wash and halve the cherries. Remove the pits. Put cherries on a deep plate.

2. Then, wash and cut strawberries into quarters. Add strawberries to the cherries.

3. Add washed blueberries.

4. Wash, cut, and peel the apple, peach, and kiwi. Add the pieces to the other ingredients.

5. Mix all fruits and berries. Pour orange juice over the fruit mixture.

6. Add two tablespoons of lemon juice. Let the salad soak up the citrus, and then drain the juice. Eat chilled.

NUTRITION

342 calories, 3g proteins, 1g fats, 52g carbs

GREEN BUCKWHEAT COFFEE CAKE

Preparation Time: 20 minutes

Cooking Time: 30 minutes

Servings: 8

INGREDIENTS

- ✓ 15 dates
- ✓ For the Filling
- ✓ 15 bright dates
- ✓ 1 cup plain milk
- ✓ For the Cake Base
- ✓ 2 tablespoons cocoa
- ✓ 1/8 cup green buckwheat
- ✓ 2 teaspoons cocoa
- ✓ 3 teaspoons chicory
- ✓ ½-1 cup milk (additional)
- ✓ 1 cup walnuts (or other to your taste)

PREPARATION

1. For the Base

2. 1.   Soak dates overnight to soften. Transfer the pits from the dates to a   food processor and blend them.
3. Peel the walnuts, and grind nuts into crumbs.
4. Add cocoa to the nuts.
5. Mix half the dates, nuts, and cocoa with a fork until smooth. Make into balls with wet hands. If the dough is too thin, add cocoa or nuts.
6. Spread the dough on the bottom of a medium middle baking sheet.

7. For the Filling
1.   Grind the green buckwheat into flour using a coffee grinder.
2.   Place the buckwheat flour in a saucepan. Pure in a bit of milk and stir well until no lumps remain.
3.   Warm up the mixture and boil until it thickens (for 5-10 minutes).
4.   Place the second half of the dates, chicory, cocoa, and a little milk in a food processor. Beat into thick, homogeneous cream. Add milk as needed.
5.   Place the mixture on top of the base. Freeze cake for 2-3 hours. If the cake is too frozen, let it stand at room temperature for 15-20 minutes.
6.   Coat the cake with the melted chocolate or icing.

NUTRITION

328 calories, 8g proteins, 19g fats, 33g carbs

PEANUT PASTE (HALVA)

Preparation Time: 10 minutes

Cooking Time: 0 minute

Servings: 10

INGREDIENTS

- ✓ 7 ounces peanuts
- ✓ 1 teaspoon vanilla sugar
- ✓ 70 ml water
- ✓ 40 ml sunflower oil
- ✓ 1/3 cup sugar
- ✓ 1/3 cup wheat flour

PREPARATION

1. Peel the peanuts. Fry in a clean and dry pan for 3-5 minutes, stirring constantly.

2. Pour the wheat flour into another pan, stirring with a spoon. Fry until creamy.

3. Remove from the heat.

4. Grind the peanuts in food processors as finely as possible.

5. Pour the fried flour into the food processor. Grind for 2 minutes.

6. Place sugar, vanilla sugar, and water in a small saucepan. Bring to a boil. Boil the syrup for one minute. Add vegetable oil, mix the ingredients, and remove from heat.

7. Pour the syrup into the peanut mixture. Mix well. The mass thickens quite quickly.

8. Put the mass into the mold. Line the form with parchment paper for easy removal. Leave the halva to cool completely.

9. The paste is ready. Cut into pieces and try!

10. Halva can be from golden to brown, depending on the degree to which the flour and peanuts are roasted.

NUTRITION

197 calories, 6g proteins, 13g fats, 11g carbs

CHAMPAGNE JELLY WITH FRUITS AND BERRIES

Preparation Time: 20 minutes

Cooking Time: 0 minute

Servings: 4

INGREDIENTS

- ✓ 500 ml semi-sweet champagne
- ✓ 2-3 apricots
- ✓ 1 medium pear
- ✓ 5 ounces strawberries
- ✓ 1 medium peach
- ✓ 5 ounces sweet cherries
- ✓ 1 medium nectarine
- ✓ 5 ounces seedless grapes
- ✓ 1/3-ounce agar-agar powder

PREPARATION

1. Wash fruits and berries well.
2. Peel the fruits and berries. Cut into pieces. Leave the grapes and other small berries for decorating.

3. Pour agar-agar into the champagne in a deep saucepan and place on low heat. Stir until the gelatin dissolves. Remove from heat.

4. Line the jelly containers with plastic wrap.

5. Place the fruits and berries in a container. Pour champagne over fruit.

6. Refrigerate for 5-6 hours. Turn the container over and remove the plastic wrap.

NUTRITION

134 calories, 2g proteins, 1g fats, 32 carbs

SPONGE CAKE

Preparation Time: 10 minutes

Cooking Time: 20 minutes

Servings: 12

INGREDIENTS

- ✓ 3 cups flour
- ✓ Three tsp. baking powder
- ✓ 1 cup olive oil
- ✓ ½ cup cornstarch
- ✓ One tsp. baking soda
- ✓ 2 cups of water
- ✓ ¼ cup lemon juice
- ✓ 2 tsp. vanilla extract
- ✓ 1 and 2/3 cup sugar
- ✓ One and ½ cup of almond milk

PREPARATION

1. In a container, mix the flour with ingredients like; cornstarch, baking powder, baking soda, and sugar and whisk well.

2. In another bowl, mix oil with almond milk, water, vanilla, and lemon juice and whisk.

3. Combine the two mixtures, stir, pour in a greased baking dish that fits your air fryer, introduce in the fryer and cook at 350 degrees F for 20 minutes.

4. Leave the cake to cool down, cut, and serve.

5. Enjoy!

NUTRITION

calories: 334 kcal, Protein: 3.32 g, Carbohydrates: 38.6 g, Fat: 18.45 g

CHOCOLATE AND POMEGRANATE BARS

Preparation Time: 120 minutes

Cooking Time: 10 minutes

Servings: 6

INGREDIENTS

- ✓ ½ cup almond milk
- ✓ 1 tsp. vanilla extract
- ✓ One and ½ cups dark chocolate, chopped
- ✓ ½ cup almonds, chopped
- ✓ ½ cup pomegranate seeds

PREPARATION

1. Heat a pan with the almond milk over medium-low heat, add chocolate, stir for 5 minutes, take off heat add vanilla extract, half of the pomegranate seeds, and half of the nuts stir.

2. Pour this into a lined baking pan, spread, sprinkle a pinch of salt, the rest of the pomegranate arils and nuts, introduce in your air fryer, and cook at 300 degrees F for 4 minutes.

3.   Keep in the fridge for 2 hours before serving.

4.   Enjoy!

<u>NUTRITION</u>

Calories 68, Fat 1g, Fiber 4g, Protein 1g, Carbs 6g.

PEACH CROCKPOT PUDDING

Preparation Time: 15 minutes

Cooking Time: 4 hours

Servings: 6

INGREDIENTS

- ✓ 2 Cups Sliced Peaches
- ✓ 1/4 Cup Maple Syrup
- ✓ 2 Cups Coconut Milk
- ✓ 1/2 Tsp. Cinnamon Powder
- ✓ For Serving
- ✓ 1 Oz. Coconut Flakes
- ✓ ½ Cup Coconut Cream

PREPARATION

1. Lightly grease the crockpot and place peaches in the bottom.
2. Add maple syrup, cinnamon powder, and milk.
3. sill the crockpot and cook on high for 4 hours.
4. Once cooked, remove from the crockpot.
5. For serving, pour coconut cream.
6. Top with coconut flakes.

CONCLUSION

The purpose of the vegan diet is to identify a diet that can be eaten by people of all dietary requirements, including those who are vegan, lactose-intolerant, or gluten-free

A vegan diet excludes meat, eggs, dairy products, and other animal products. A vegan lifestyle also avoids wearing clothing made from animals' fur or killed for leather production. Veganism is a moral philosophy and lifestyle seeking to exclude the use of animals for food as much as possible. It maintains that the use of products made from or by animals is a form of speciesism, similar to racism.

The primary sources of vegan foods are whole grains, legumes, seeds, nuts, fruits, and vegetables. Also, must be included a multitude of vitamins to the needed daily requirement.

The vegan diet is also deficient in cholesterol and high in fiber content. You have to eat, also, fiber-rich food such as lentils and beans.

Those who want to follow a vegan diet must ensure they get sufficient amounts of omega 6 and omega 3 fatty acids, which can be found in flax seeds, walnuts, or chia seeds 3s; and walnuts, sunflower seeds, or pumpkin seeds for omega 6s. Dairy products are also not suitable if following a vegan diet as they do not allow for these essential fats.

If you decide to go vegan, ensure you also take a multivitamin supplement. Another way to ensure your body gets the correct amount of nutrients is to eat raw foods, which are more nutrient-dense than cooked ones. Eating natural foods means that you can digest them more efficiently, and they contain more enzymes and vitamins.

A healthy vegan diet will be low in fats and sugars, but it can be high in fiber. A vegan diet should also include a wide variety of food. It is a mistake to base your intake on only one type of fruit or vegetable, as you will miss out on essential nutrients if you do this. The vegan diet is healthy because it promotes a healthy lifestyle.

CPSIA information can be obtained
at www.ICGtesting.com
Printed in the USA
BVHW091036030521
606322BV00002B/278